OBLIQUE MUSIC

A Book of Hours

OBLIQUE MUSIC

A Book of Hours

tanka by
Elizabeth Bodien

Shanti Arts Publishing
Brunswick, Maine

Oblique Music: A Book of Hours

Published by Shanti Arts Publishing
Interior and cover design by Shanti Arts Designs

Cover and interior image from Magnilion
/ istockphoto.com / 165681323

Shanti Arts LLC
193 Hillside Road
Brunswick, Maine 04011
www.shantiarts.com

Printed in the United States of America

ISBN: 978-1-947067-70-7

Library of Congress Control Number: 2018967071

for Tamsin

DAWN

a thick snow
of cherry blossoms
fell in the night
floating to blankets
where we dreamers slept

I dreamt of you
from our long ago
that smile
how it intoxicates
even after long years

now these blossoms

in brand new light

open

what is possible

anything anything

I feel long

when I wake up

was it the night?

did I travel great years?

move through many species?

lingering in bed
one moment longer
I trawl
the vast in-between
where creation might stir

your voice

so gravelly

this morning

what roads did you

travel in your sleep?

as night begins
to relinquish its darkness
I cannot remember
the view from any window
save that of my childhood

morning fog softens
the hard angles of barns
sunlight sifts in
the day opens smooth
my own corners relax

we enter

the day as we find it

as if in a dream

this morning —

fog

I lose myself
in the breathing of fog
edges blur
if I dissolve
will I emerge?

EARLY MORNING

blue-gray light
and silhouetted trees
of early morning —
    a woodcut, inked and ready
    to press onto a blank day

in dim light now
we untangle ourselves
to this day's music
its unmet surprises
sorrows and blessings

cold morning
her old rug
by my bed now
I step into the life
she left behind

downy clouds

on dawn's horizon

rise up

against a doomsday sky

yielding to light

first sun

on the gnarly sycamore

ghostly white

a whisper of color

between dark and day

furrowed bark
of the butternut tree
in morning light
I wish my wrinkles
would look as wise

an array of trees
edged in gold leaf
by sun
I want to bathe
in that brimming light

on a box elder leaf
backlit by the sun
the shadow of a fly
crawls, lifts away
I ponder flight

a huge spider web
between ground and willow
shimmers in sunlight
an opus in progress
till a cowbird flies through it

after her passing
I drive Mother's car
through the seasons
in the rearview mirror
her face

I'm fooled each time
I pass by that stump
looking so human
does some kindly spirit
find its home there?

a life entire

in the swoop of a blackbird

wing flash of red

sufficient this morning

for a rising up of wonder

LATE MORNING

white pear blossoms
festive as popcorn
strung along branches
surprise after surprise
they burst open like song

under the oak trees

three thoughts as I stroll . . .

one is of you

the second of me

the best is of us

Queen Anne's Lace
surrounds where I walk
such a greeting
how might I respond
in the language of flowers?

the sharp point
of this pencil
ready for paper
invites me to write
— what words are waiting?

how could a painter
portray this on canvas —
this froth of green
the madness of new leaves
after spring rain?

woodpecker:
the red on your head
fixes my gaze
until you fly away
I must let go

we peer
from the bus
across the river
our final destination
the city veiled in mist

I relish
for today
being unknown
no one in this city
can call me by name

a fish-and-chips sky
looking seaside and worn
a sotto voce day
I ask nothing of it
it asks nothing of me

warm day

the air feels old-fashioned

no need to hurry

what moves moves slowly

what does not stays at rest

MIDDAY

after gray days
at last brilliant sunshine
warm on the skin
as the plants do
I lean toward the light

to step out now
without grabbing a coat
like childhood
airy, wide open
no endings in sight

four old women
gather in spring
at their friend's grave
by the whispering sea
humming the same tune

her voice

sings a Handel aria

like a bird

I soar

rising . . . rising . . .

clouds line up
in rows across the sky
like questions
are there any answers
or just endless gray?

under an easy sky
a man on a red tractor
in tawny fields
mows and turns, mows and turns
in a seed of perfection

outside her door
a woman trims bushes
with aplomb
    after the growing
    the cutting back

July cicada
splits open its shell
here on a bean leaf
    oh, the changes, the changes
    asked or unasked for

worry

is a hungry creature

it feeds

on wayward thoughts

and idle imaginings

rapt, I listen
to Albinoni's Adagio
and weep
soft tremblings
of a willow in breeze

I buy cut tulips
arrange them in a vase
for their color
and because I trust
they will be here tomorrow

in cerulean sky
white clouds puff up
as longing rises
could we fly together
climb over the clouds?

EARLY AFTERNOON

clouds so low
they seem to tumble
close over head
let them do the racing
I will just watch

rain, I can smell you
a blessing down the valley
coming this way
my arms open wide
I wait for your wetness

at the burial
the urn of ashes
so small
no match for the memories
of so many years

she saved the dress

for this somber occasion

wondering

how she would change

within its granite shades

cleaning the closet
I find the comforter
you knit for me
    even on this summer day
    I wrap myself in it

clouds pile on clouds
playing King-of-the-Castle
or so it seems
under this rollicking sky
I could go reckless

high on the barn roof
lightning rods twitch
one hulking crow
a tremor of air
a trace of danger

weather report:
tornado, take cover!
instead I go out
without you, to bellow
at the yellowing sky

spring to summer
these gaps between your calls
I fill with worry
seasons have not changed
my love for you

the sight
of you waiting
at the airport
is all I need
to feel home

LATE AFTERNOON

heavy non-stop rain
beach vacation spoiled
inside, we look out
eat bowls of popcorn
fall into each other's naps

the boy flies his kite
a terrible, red-nosed tengu
ferocious winds
twisting and turning
the dreaming child wakes

barely touching
his scraped bloody knee
the boy ponders
for the first time
what is inside him

he says, I miss my friends
from my old school
I must start over
like trees, Grandma says
making new leaves each year

iridescent blue
two dragonflies
catch and throw
waning sunlight
onto the path

a forest of leaf buds

through summer's profusion

in autumn colors

all that growing

falls to the ground

I travel alone
this rust autumn day
my eyes alive
without conversation
I hear the wind shifting

a maze of rooms

in this strange roofless building

endless tangles

how to find the way

my only guide this wind

air turning cold
autumn's blaze of color
almost gone
the way your voice sounded
I don't want to forget

puffed up
against the cold
the sparrow
beats its small wings
even faster

black-necked geese
pepper the hillside
this dull afternoon
I stop mourning the dead
make a hot soup for winter

cows lie close
to ground in the field
rain coming
our moods and moves shift
as weather turns

EVENING

the old well
empty of water
enchants
as a portal
into deep earth

smoke rises

from the burning barrel

our trash

turns to ash, to air

what will we become?

just for today
let's not talk of death
look at the forest
some trees are falling
but so many rise up

triplet sunbeams
fall through the window
oblique music
in a key that keeps shifting
playing my mood

violin and cello
each chase a melody
across afternoon
like a long-married couple
in on-and-off harmony

no one knows
how great love can be
until within it
lover and beloved
cannot tell which is which

colors at dusk

mute into grayness

not like life fading

I intend to grow sharper

to landscapes that matter

the sun itself
seems reluctant to set
on such an evening
its rosy light lingers
on high hemlock branches

a silent snow
cool bits of heaven
melt on my skin
I could stay here forever
just for the feel of it

this night
under the bowl of heaven
I gaze upward
small, but enlarged
by magnificent starshine

yellow light
calls from the windows
as I trudge home
snow swirls around me
right up to the door

quiet settles

in dusky shadows

so do I

feeling at one

with my surround

NIGHT

tonight I ache
for the young woman I was
who was she?
enduring still like rock
or vanished in wind?

at my window
diminishing light
as on any day
I fend off the thought
of my own fading

full moon —
howling in the dark forest
a lone coyote
in my white lace gown
I step out, join in

if I were to choose

a picture of your kindness:

your smile

as you gave up your coat

that chill winter night

discovered inside

a ragged book of poems

your letter

I still can recite

your words by heart

grandmother
brushes and braids her hair
for the night
the moon in her window
all hum in silver

the moon's side
that we never see
    what we say
    what we want to say
    not the same

reading the old words

the Book of Common Prayer

I am lifted

to some place where

all is meet and right

filmy curtains
usher in the night wind
fragrant with spirits
the house with its sleepers
dreams of the dead

I throw off

winter blankets

too heavy

the space beside me

where you used to sleep

like soft cotton
a night breeze wafts through
descants above
bass notes of earth
as we sleep between

the last train
pulls out of the station
at midnight
window lights and stars
merge in the distance

BEYOND

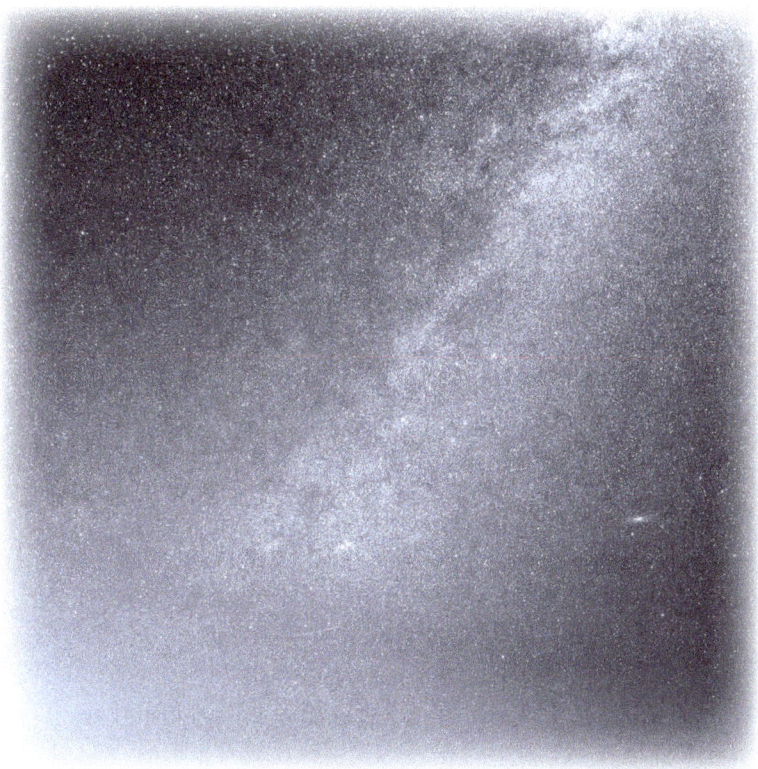

your breathing stops
my breath follows yours
a refrain
the nurse opens a window
you leave on a breeze

broken goblet

where we kept

small change

I can't ask you now

from where it came

an old game
among your belongings
the cards dog-eared
your hands that held them
do so no longer

since your death

your house under sycamores

for sale, rooms empty

I can see through

to the other side

we are all old
now that you've gone
you danced
like a butterfly
on the lid of our lives

what was her name?
the one crossing the fields
to bring us good news?
she walked as if peace
breathed out from her limbs

inland
I longed for the sea
the waves
a blue invitation
to forever and ever

I pulled and pulled
my heavy line from the sea
surprised to find
the weight of history
myself tangled in it

frost flickers
on the dark window
a thin veil
separates this earth
from beyond

snow so deep
everything is hidden
I will sleep now
wake up sometime
in spring

oh, to sleep well
the whirr of the earth
lullaby-like
humming low in the ear
for we dark side ones

between
the dying and the living
a blue valley widens
on one side, towards sleep
the other, towards dawn

ACKNOWLEDGMENTS

Grateful acknowledgment is made to the following journals where these tanka appeared in their original versions:

a forest of leaf buds, *GUSTS: Contemporary Tanka*, Fall/Winter 2016

a life entire, *Atlas Poetica*, Autumn 2012

a huge spider web, *Atlas Poetica 30*, 2017

a maze of rooms, *red lights*, January 2011

a perfect snow, *red lights*, January 2013

a thick snow, *red lights*, June 2015

after her passing, *red lights*, January 2015

after gray days, *Magnapoets 9*, January 2012

air turning cold, *red lights*, January 2009

an array of trees, *GUSTS: Contemporary Tanka*, Spring/Summer 2012

an old game, *Modern English Tanka*, Summer 2009

as night began, *red lights*, June 2015

at my window, *Take Five: Best Contemporary Tanka Vol. 4*, May 2012

at the burial, *GUSTS: Contemporary Tanka*, Fall/Winter 2016

between the dying and the living, *red lights*, June 2010

black-necked geese, *GUSTS: Contemporary Tanka*, Spring/Summer 2012

blue-gray light, *GUSTS: Contemporary Tanka*, Spring/Summer 2012

broken goblet, *red lights*, June 2008

cleaning the closet, *Ribbons*, Winter 2012

clouds line up, *bottle rockets 26*, February 2012

clouds pile on clouds, *American Tanka*, June 2012

clouds so low, *red lights*, January 2011

cold morning, *Wisteria*, April 2009

colors at dusk, *Magnapoets*, January 2011

discovered inside, *GUSTS: Contemporary Tanka*, Fall/
    Winter 2017

downy clouds, *red lights*, January 2015

filmy curtains, *GUSTS: Contemporary Tanka*, Fall/Winter 2014

first sun, *red lights*, June 2017

four old women, *Modern English Tanka*, Summer 2009

full moon, *Modern English Tanka*, Summer 2009

grandmother, *Modern English Tanka*, Summer 2009

(he says) I miss my friends, *Atlas Poetica: Special Issue for
    Children*, February 2011

heavy non-stop rain, *red lights*, January 2006

her voice, *GUSTS: Contemporary Tanka*, Fall/Winter 2012

high on the barn roof, *Atlas Poetica*, Autumn 2012

how could a painter, *GUSTS: Contemporary Tanka*, Spring/
    Summer 2013

I buy cut tulips, *Ribbons*, Spring/Summer 2012

I dreamt of you, *red lights*, June 2013

I feel long, *red lights*, January 2013

(I like this) warm day, *GUSTS: Contemporary Tanka*,
    Spring/Summer 2013

I lose myself, *red lights,* January 2014

I pulled and pulled, *GUSTS: Contemporary Tanka,* Fall/
    Winter 2011

I relish, *Tanka Society of America Anthology,* 2017

I travel alone, *American Tanka 18,* December 2010

I throw off, *red lights,* January 2009

if I were to choose, *Modern English Tanka,* Summer 2009

in dim light now, *GUSTS: Contemporary Tanka,* Spring/
    Summer 2015

inland, *Ribbons,* Winter 2010

iridescent blue, *Eucalypt* (Australia), November 2010

July cicada, *red lights,* June 2017

just for today, *red lights,* June 2012

lingering in bed, *GUSTS: Contemporary Tanka,* Fall/
    Winter 2013

morning fog softens, *Atlas Poetica,* Autumn 2012

no one knows, *GUSTS: Contemporary Tanka,* Fall/
    Winter 2011

now these blossoms, *red lights,* June 2015

on a box elder leaf, *red lights,* January 2018

puffed up from "Into the Cold", *red lights,* January 2017

Queen Anne's Lace, *Atlas Poetica,* Autumn 2012

rain, I can smell you, *GUSTS: Contemporary Tanka*, Fall/ Winter 2011

reading the old words, *Modern English Tanka*, Summer 2009

she saved the dress, *GUSTS: Contemporary Tanka*, Fall/ Winter 2014

since your death, *Tanka Society of America Anthology*, 2010

snow so deep, *red lights*, January 2010

spring to summer, *Modern English Tanka*, Summer 2009

the boy flies his kite, *red lights*, January 2012

the furrowed bark, *Modern English Tanka*, Summer 2009

the last train, *red lights*, January 2016

the old well, *GUSTS: Contemporary Tanka*, Spring/ Summer 2016

the sharp point, *Modern English Tanka*, Summer 2009

the sight, *GUSTS: Contemporary Tanka*, Fall/Winter 2013

the sun itself, *red lights*, June 2014

this night, *red lights*, January 2016

to step out now, *red lights*, June 2014

triplet sunbeams, *red lights*, June 2013

under an easy sky (easy skies), *Atlas Poetica*, Autumn 2012

under the oak trees, *red lights*, January 2018

violin and cello, *GUSTS: Contemporary Tanka*, Fall/Winter 2012

we are all old from "Into the Cold", *red lights*, January 2017

we enter, *red lights*, June 2012

weather report, *red lights*, January 2010

what was her name? *Magnapoets 9*, January 2012

white pear blossoms, *GUSTS: Contemporary Tanka*, Spring/
 Summer 2013

woodpecker, *Ribbons*, Spring 2009

worry, *red lights*, January 2014

yellow light, *Ribbons*, Winter, 2009

your breathing stops, *red lights*, June 2009

your voice, *Modern English Tanka*, Summer 2009

ABOUT THE AUTHOR

photo: Elaine Zelker, LLC

ELIZABETH BODIEN grew up in the "burned-over" district of western New York State, but now lives near Hawk Mountain, Pennsylvania. She holds degrees in cultural anthropology, consciousness studies, religions, and poetry. She has worked as an instructor of English in Japan; an organic farmer in the mountains of Oregon; a childbirth instructor in Ghana, West Africa; and as a professor of anthropology. Her poems, essays, and book reviews have appeared in *Cimarron Review, Crannóg*, and *Parabola*, among many other publications in the United States, Ireland, Canada, Australia, and India. Her collections are: *Plumb Lines; Rough Terrain: Notes of an Undutiful Daughter*, which is about her mother's decline with Alzheimer's; *Endpapers; I Sing the Undersung*; and *Blood, Metal, Fiber, Rock*. She has appeared on television and radio and taught workshops on poetry and poetics. Currently she is working on a collection of her trance writings.

• www.elizabethbodien.com